I0867546

# Would You Rather?

## Sports

EDITION

# Would You Rather?

## Sports

EDITION

Play Ball with a Hilarious Game
of Slam Dunk Scenarios

LINDSEY DALY

Z KIDS • NEW YORK

Published in the United States by Z Kids, an imprint of Zeitgeist™
A division of Penguin Random House LLC
1745 Broadway, New York, NY 10019
penguinrandomhouse.com
zeitgeistpublishing.com



ISBN: 9780593886090

Ebook ISBN: 9780593885956

Cover art © by Olga Ermakova/Shutterstock.com, Vector_Bird/Shutterstock.com, LineSolution/Shutterstock.com
Interior art © mhatzapa/Shutterstock.com, JosepPerianes/Shutterstock.com, Kusumailustration/Shutterstock.com, redgreystock/Shutterstock.com, Yuliya Marholina/Shutterstock.com, LineSolution/Shutterstock.com, jesadaphorn/Shutterstock.com, Freud/Shutterstock.com, mentalmind/Shutterstock.com, Tamim 99Graphics/Shutterstock.com
Book design by Erin Yeung
Author photograph © by Jocelyn Morales

Printed in the United States of America
The authorized representative in the EU for product safety and compliance is Penguin Random House Ireland, Morrison Chambers, 32 Nassau Street, Dublin D02 YH68, Ireland. https://eu-contact.penguin.ie
2nd Printing

For Mom and Dad—my biggest cheerleaders—
and for the Unity Wolves volleyball team

# Contents

# Introduction

Whether you're cheering as a spectator, comparing team stats, or getting in the game yourself, almost everyone enjoys the thrill of sports. Need to pass time waiting for a table at a restaurant or on a long road trip (maybe to a soccer tournament)? *Would You Rather? Sports Edition* offers more than 160 questions about the exciting world of athletics.

These "Would You Rather?" questions are an excellent way to showcase your knowledge of all things sports related and are designed to start funny, thoughtful, and creative discussions. The questions are for kids ages 8–12 but they're sure to entertain the whole family. You never know what fascinating details you might learn about what and *how* other people think!

*Would You Rather? Sports Edition* can be played as a game with winners for individual questions and rounds based on humor, logic, and overall creativity. In this book, you'll find funny and thought-provoking scenarios revolving around the sports that spark passion and joy all over the world. Are you up to the challenge of stretching your imagination and putting your mind to the test? Get ready to show off your critical thinking skills, have fun, and become the champion of wits while playing *Would You Rather? Sports Edition!*

# Rules of the Game

Get a group of friends or family members together for a game of wits and creativity. The more the better!

* The game is played in eight rounds, with twenty questions in each round.
* Players rotate the responsibility of being the "judge" and read the question aloud to the group.
* Players will then respond with an explanation and take turns sharing their answers.
* The judge of that round will choose the best answer based on humor, creativity, or logic. Write the winner's name in the space provided below the question and assign them one point. If only two people are playing, the judge (the player reading the question) assigns 1 to 5 points for the answer (5 being the best answer) and records it with the

other player's name in the space provided below the question.

* When all players complete the round, tally up the points to determine the winner for that round.
* In the event of a tie at the end of a round, the players who are tied will answer the tiebreaker question. All remaining players will vote on the best answer. If only two people are playing, whoever makes the other player laugh wins.
* When all players complete the book, the winner of the most rounds is the champion!

# ROUND 1

# Go Team!

**Would you rather**

play soccer on crutches

**or**

basketball with a cast on your arm?

WINNER: POINTS:

**Would you rather**

wear a fishbowl as a football helmet

**or**

a flowerpot?

WINNER: POINTS:

**Would you rather**
be the soccer goalie in
a penalty shootout
**or**
the kicker?

WINNER: POINTS:

**Would you rather**
have impressive personal stats
but few team wins
**or**
little individual success on
a championship team?

WINNER: POINTS:

**Would you rather**

be able to slam-dunk

**or**

hit a home run?

WINNER: POINTS:

**Would you rather**

have baseball mitts for hands

**or**

hockey sticks?

WINNER: POINTS:

**Would you rather**
play soccer in thick mud
**or**
knee-high water?

WINNER: POINTS:

**Would you rather**
miss the winning field goal
**or**
strike out in the final inning?

WINNER: POINTS:

**Would you rather**

have a hockey puck for a nose

**or**

a pickleball?

WINNER: POINTS:

**Would you rather**

sleep on an outdoor basketball court

**or**

in a baseball dugout?

WINNER: POINTS:

**Would you rather**

play soccer wearing flip-flops

**or**

ice hockey barefoot?

WINNER: POINTS:

**Would you rather**

get cut from the team

**or**

sit on the bench all season?

WINNER: POINTS:

**Would you rather**
use a tennis ball in place
of a football
**or**
a boomerang?

WINNER: POINTS:

**Would you rather**
collide with the catcher
sliding into home
**or**
headbutt a defensive lineman?

WINNER: POINTS:

**Would you rather**

get your tooth knocked out
playing ice hockey

**or**

break your finger playing
baseball?

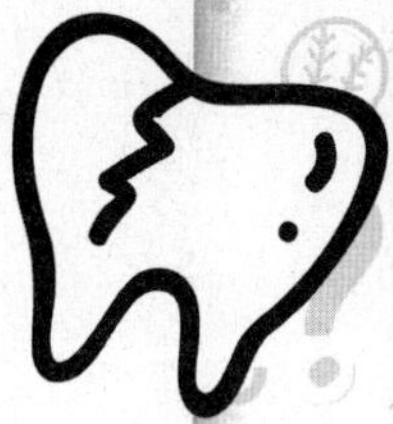

WINNER: POINTS:

**Would you rather**

sink multiple three-pointers
in a basketball game

**or**

win every jump ball?

WINNER: POINTS:

**Would you rather**
be the highest scorer
on your team
**or**
voted captain by your
teammates?

WINNER: POINTS:

**Would you rather**
use a soccer ball as a pillow
**or**
a football?

WINNER: POINTS:

**Would you rather**
play hockey on a melting ice rink
**or**
football in a blizzard?

WINNER: POINTS:

**Would you rather**
use a lacrosse stick as
a baseball bat
**or**
as a hockey stick?

WINNER: POINTS:

## TIEBREAKER

**Would you rather**

get hit by a fast pitch

**or**

a hockey puck?

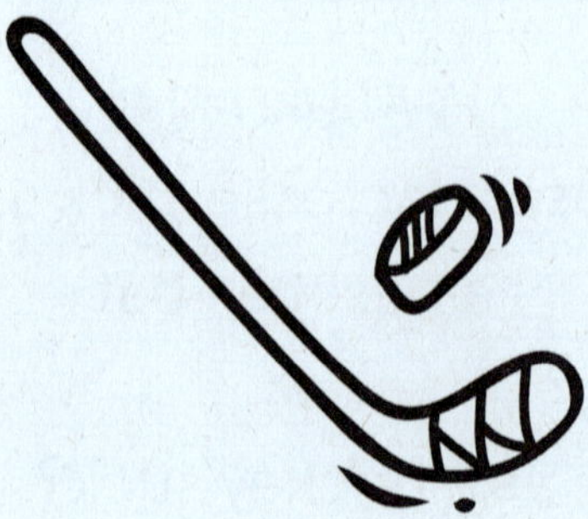

WINNER: POINTS:

WINNER: ______________________________

TOTAL POINTS: ______________________________

# ROUND

# 2

# Solo Sports

**Would you rather**

lose control of your horse during a competition

**or**

slip off the diving board?

WINNER: POINTS:

**Would you rather**

play a round of mini golf using a wooden spoon as a club

**or**

an umbrella?

WINNER: POINTS:

**Would you rather**

forget your choreography

**or**

make an error during your tumbling routine?

WINNER: POINTS:

**Would you rather**

get a cramp in the middle of a footrace

**or**

have to go to the bathroom?

WINNER: POINTS:

**Would you rather**

compete in a pool filled with ice

**or**

set to 100 degrees?

WINNER: POINTS:

**Would you rather**

be a skilled archer

**or**

equestrian?

WINNER: POINTS:

**Would you rather**

have a tennis court in your backyard

**or**

an Olympic-size swimming pool?

WINNER: POINTS:

**Would you rather**

wear a swim cap for a year

**or**

goggles?

WINNER: POINTS:

**Would you rather**

have tennis balls for feet

**or**

golf clubs for legs?

WINNER: POINTS:

**Would you rather**

bowl a perfect game

**or**

get a bull's-eye in archery?

WINNER: POINTS:

**Would you rather**

be a competitive bull rider

**or**

show jump horses?

WINNER: POINTS:

**Would you rather**

create a new gymnastics move during practice

**or**

stick a perfect landing in a competition?

WINNER: POINTS:

**Would you rather**

the music stopped in the middle of your dance routine

**or**

dance to a song you haven't practiced?

WINNER: POINTS:

**Would you rather**

compete in a swim meet wearing a snowsuit

**or**

nothing at all?

WINNER: POINTS:

**Would you rather**
win at the national level
**or**
lose at the Olympics?

WINNER: POINTS:

**Would you rather**
compete in a tennis match
in the pouring rain
**or**
during a heat wave?

WINNER: POINTS:

**Would you rather**

be the best weight lifter
in your age group

**or**

the best skateboarder?

WINNER: POINTS:

**Would you rather**

use a shovel as a tennis racket

**or**

as a lacrosse stick?

WINNER: POINTS:

**Would you rather**
complete a triathlon with a painful blister
**or**
a traditional marathon with shin splints?

WINNER: POINTS:

**Would you rather**
go kayaking without a paddle
**or**
mountain biking with broken gears?

WINNER: POINTS:

# TIEBREAKER

**Would you rather**

play tennis with soccer balls

**or**

Ping-Pong balls?

WINNER: POINTS:

WINNER

WINNER: ____________________

TOTAL POINTS: ____________________

# ROUND 3

# Only the Best

**Would you rather**

be a referee at the World Cup

**or**

the Super Bowl?

WINNER: POINTS:

**Would you rather**

be seated at the World Series next to someone who keeps sneezing on you

**or**

farting?

WINNER: POINTS:

**Would you rather**
be the fastest runner on earth
**or**
the highest jumper?

WINNER: POINTS:

**Would you rather**
win a marathon without drinking any water
**or**
on a full stomach?

WINNER: POINTS:

**Would you rather**
watch your favorite team win the Super Bowl
**or**
lose but meet them after the game?

WINNER: POINTS:

**Would you rather**
watch half of the World Cup championship in person
**or**
the whole game on TV?

WINNER: POINTS:

**Would you rather**
win a marathon as one of only two runners
**or**
place second out of 100 runners?

WINNER: POINTS:

**Would you rather**
have an athletic move named after you
**or**
a championship trophy?

WINNER: POINTS:

**Would you rather**
come in last place in a championship race
**or**
get injured before the race?

WINNER: POINTS:

**Would you rather**
win the Little League World Series with your team
**or**
win an individual title in track and field?

WINNER: POINTS:

**Would you rather**
hold the record for most home runs
**or**
most saves as a goalie?

WINNER: POINTS:

**Would you rather**
be the best athlete at school but hated
**or**
the worst athlete but loved?

WINNER: POINTS:

**Would you rather**
share the Stanley Cup with
your teammates
**or**
win your own
lesser-known trophy?

WINNER: POINTS:

**Would you rather**
have a Super Bowl ring that's
too small for your finger
**or**
a cracked Olympic gold medal?

WINNER: POINTS:

**Would you rather**

be the strongest person on your team

**or**

the most strategic?

WINNER: POINTS:

**Would you rather**

be the most skilled NASCAR driver with the worst car

**or**

an average driver with the most equipped car?

WINNER: POINTS:

**Would you rather**
catch a foul ball at the World Series
**or**
shake hands with your favorite player?

WINNER: POINTS:

**Would you rather**
win the Kentucky Derby
**or**
the Formula 1 Grand Prix?

WINNER: POINTS:

**Would you rather**

have a long career as a mid-tier player

**or**

a short career as a superstar?

WINNER: POINTS:

**Would you rather**

play for the most hated team in the league

**or**

the least talented?

WINNER: POINTS:

## TIEBREAKER

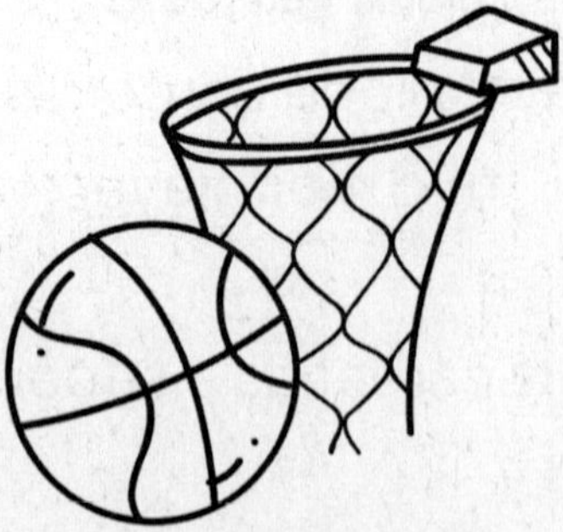

**Would you rather**

play in March Madness

**or**

drive a race car in the Daytona 500?

WINNER: POINTS:

# WINNER

WINNER: ______________________________

TOTAL POINTS: ______________________________

# ROUND

# 4

# What's New?

**Would you rather**

be blindfolded while skateboarding

**or**

rock climbing?

WINNER: POINTS:

**Would you rather**

be the smallest player on your rugby team

**or**

the slowest?

WINNER: POINTS:

**Would you rather**
be the best athlete in
a new, ignored sport
**or**
the worst athlete in a popular,
traditional sport?

WINNER: POINTS:

**Would you rather**
be a black belt in karate
**or**
a professional snowboarder?

WINNER: POINTS:

**Would you rather**
play Ping-Pong using
a kayak paddle
**or**
a hockey stick?

WINNER: POINTS:

**Would you rather**
wear boxing gloves
while rock climbing
**or**
perform a cheer routine
on stilts?

WINNER: POINTS:

**Would you rather**
ski down a mountain
of quicksand
**or**
mud?

WINNER: POINTS:

**Would you rather**
enter a breakdancing contest
with zero experience
**or**
a skateboarding competition?

WINNER: POINTS:

**Would you rather**

accidentally drop the flier

on your cheer squad

**or**

kick your karate sensei?

WINNER: POINTS:

**Would you rather**

have a Ping-Pong table

in your classroom

**or**

a pickleball court?

WINNER: POINTS:

**Would you rather**
snowboard down a double black diamond
**or**
go heli-skiing?

WINNER: POINTS:

**Would you rather**
go rock climbing without a harness
**or**
skiing without poles?

WINNER: POINTS:

**Would you rather**

be an NFL cheerleader

**or**

on the first ever Olympic cheer team?

WINNER: POINTS:

**Would you rather**

ride a skateboard with bicycle wheels

**or**

car tires?

WINNER: POINTS:

**Would you rather**
invent a new sport
**or**
learn from athletes in
a popular sport?

WINNER: POINTS:

**Would you rather**
win a silver medal in skateboarding
at the Olympics
**or**
come in first place in BMX racing
at the X Games?

WINNER: POINTS:

**Would you rather**

compete in a race on a bicycle without brakes

**or**

on a long board that's missing a wheel?

WINNER: POINTS:

**Would you rather**

coach the Ping-Pong team

**or**

the cheer squad?

WINNER: POINTS:

**Would you rather**

go rock climbing in a dangerous, remote location

**or**

a safe but crowded spot?

WINNER: POINTS:

**Would you rather**

have a half-pipe for skateboarding in your backyard

**or**

multiple jumps and rails?

WINNER: POINTS:

## TIEBREAKER

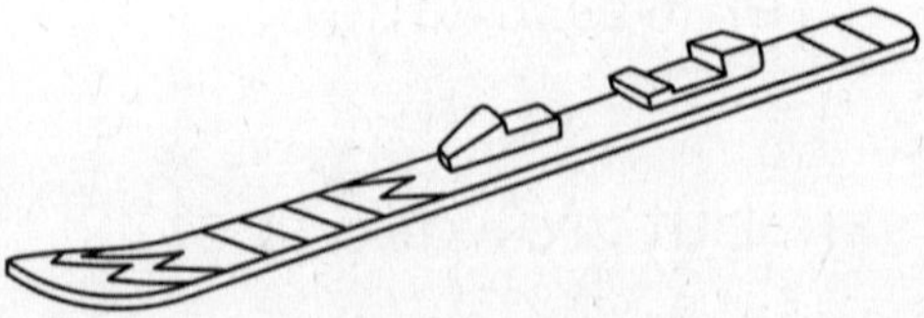

**Would you rather**

fly down a mountain
on one ski

**or**

on a snowboard without
foot bindings?

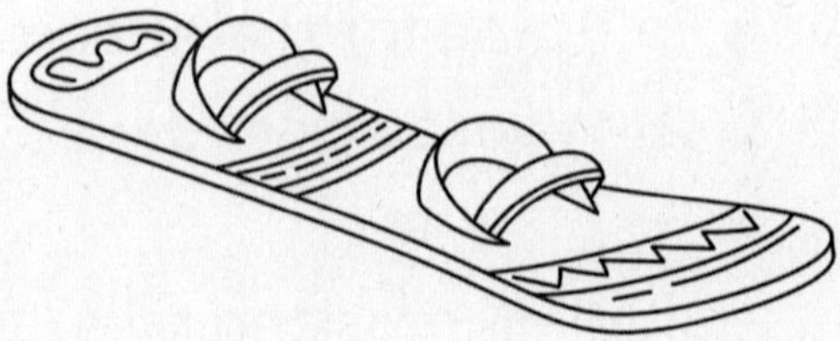

WINNER: POINTS:

WINNER: ____________________

TOTAL POINTS: ____________________

# ROUND 5

# In Season

**Would you rather**

Rollerblade on a sandy beach

**or**

a sheet of ice?

WINNER: POINTS:

**Would you rather**

teach a toddler how to play lacrosse

**or**

an elderly person?

WINNER: POINTS:

**Would you rather**

capsize your sailboat

**or**

fall off your surfboard while riding a wave?

WINNER: POINTS:

**Would you rather**

play beach volleyball on scorching hot sand

**or**

snow?

WINNER: POINTS:

**Would you rather**
drive a dogsled
**or**
be a passenger?

WINNER: POINTS:

**Would you rather**
have a pimple the size of
a baseball on your face
**or**
the size of a volleyball
on your back?

WINNER: POINTS:

**Would you rather**
hit the winning home run
**or**
win by catching your opponent's fly ball?

WINNER: POINTS:

**Would you rather**
be the captain of your baseball team
**or**
a coach?

WINNER: POINTS:

**Would you rather**

attend an outdoor yoga retreat in the winter

**or**

a fitness bootcamp in the desert?

WINNER: POINTS:

**Would you rather**

play volleyball using a pumpkin

**or**

an apple?

WINNER: POINTS:

**Would you rather**

catch a wave on your surfboard facing the opposite direction

**or**

ski backward down a mountain?

WINNER: POINTS:

**Would you rather**

compete on a summer swim team that races in a swamp

**or**

a river?

WINNER: POINTS:

**Would you rather**
play roller hockey on
a cobblestone street
**or**
gravel?

WINNER: POINTS:

**Would you rather**
realize you have motion sickness
after you join a sailing team
**or**
a fear of heights as you jump
out of an airplane?

WINNER: POINTS:

**Would you rather**
camp on a baseball field
**or**
at the top of a ski mountain?

WINNER: POINTS:

**Would you rather**
play water polo in a pool filled with water snakes
**or**
catfish?

WINNER: POINTS:

**Would you rather**
wear ice skates during
a cross-country race
**or**
Rollerblades to your
soccer game?

WINNER: POINTS:

**Would you rather**
captain a sailboat
with no training
**or**
a dogsled?

WINNER: POINTS:

**Would you rather**
sled down a sand dune in a laundry basket
**or**
a cardboard box?

WINNER: POINTS:

**Would you rather**
be stuck on a chairlift at a ski resort
**or**
on a surfboard in the ocean?

WINNER: POINTS:

## TIEBREAKER

**Would you rather**

ski in a bathing suit

**or**

surf in a winter coat?

WINNER: POINTS:

# WINNER

WINNER: ______________________________

TOTAL POINTS: ______________________________

# ROUND 6

# Wait, There's More!

**Would you rather**
be the alternate on a
four-person curling team
**or**
a fifteen-person rugby team?

WINNER: POINTS:

**Would you rather**
bowl three strikes in a game
**or**
six spares?

WINNER: POINTS:

**Would you rather**
be the tallest person on
your volleyball team
**or**
the best server?

WINNER: POINTS:

**Would you rather**
be in the heaviest wrestling
weight class
**or**
the lightest?

WINNER: POINTS:

**Would you rather**

compete against your best friend in a boxing match

**or**

your worst enemy?

WINNER: POINTS:

**Would you rather**

wear a fencing mask every day for a month

**or**

bowling shoes for a year?

WINNER: POINTS:

**Would you rather**

perform your synchronized swimming routine with your eyes closed

**or**

your gymnastics routine?

WINNER: POINTS:

**Would you rather**

be the most famous cricket player

**or**

the least famous baseball player?

WINNER: POINTS:

**Would you rather**
compete against a bodybuilder in an arm wrestling match
**or**
play handball against a professional baseball pitcher?

WINNER: POINTS:

**Would you rather**
be responsible for steering your rowing team's boat
**or**
providing the power for it to move?

WINNER: POINTS:

**Would you rather**

play darts using chopsticks

**or**

butter knives?

WINNER: POINTS:

**Would you rather**

serve an ace in volleyball

**or**

spike on your opponent?

WINNER: POINTS:

**Would you rather**

learn how to curl

**or**

play squash?

WINNER: POINTS:

**Would you rather**

get hit by a stray paintball

**or**

dart?

WINNER: POINTS:

**Would you rather**
compete against a rugby team with a strong offense and weak defense
**or**
a solid defense and a weak offense?

WINNER: POINTS:

**Would you rather**
play an Ultimate Frisbee game in front of a large uninterested crowd
**or**
a few dedicated fans?

WINNER: POINTS:

**Would you rather**

wrestle someone who has a rash

**or**

is covered in sweat?

WINNER: POINTS:

**Would you rather**

be a fencer with fast reflexes

**or**

impressive accuracy?

WINNER: POINTS:

**Would you rather**
dominate the opposing lacrosse team
**or**
make a dramatic comeback to win in the final quarter?

WINNER: POINTS:

**Would you rather**
be the least experienced member of your badminton team
**or**
a veteran member responsible for teaching the new kids?

WINNER: POINTS:

## TIEBREAKER

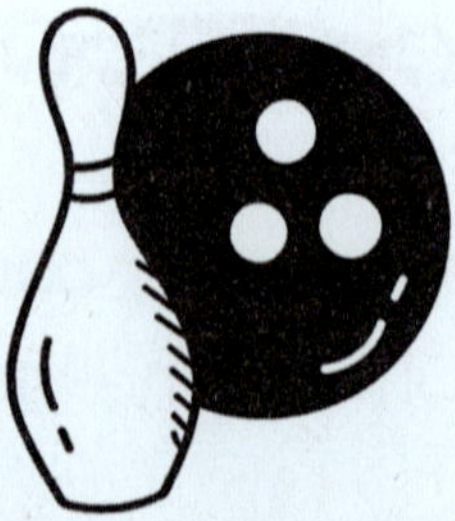

**Would you rather**

bowl with a 40-pound ball

**or**

wear slippery socks?

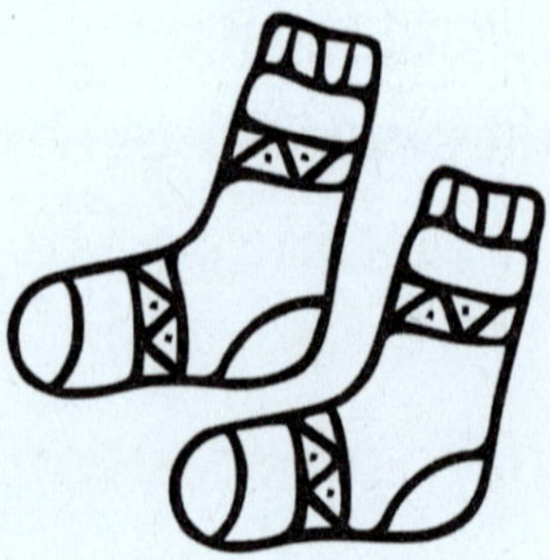

WINNER: POINTS:

## WINNER

WINNER: ______________________________

TOTAL POINTS: ______________________________

# ROUND 7

# Gold-Medal Games

**Would you rather**

win one gold medal

**or**

three silver medals?

WINNER: POINTS:

**Would you rather**

get injured right before going to the Olympics

**or**

narrowly miss making the team?

WINNER: POINTS:

**Would you rather**
compete in bobsledding as a two-person team
**or**
a four-person team?

WINNER: POINTS:

**Would you rather**
win bronze against the best athletes in the world
**or**
gold without any real competition?

WINNER: POINTS:

**Would you rather**

be eliminated from the 100-meter dash for getting a false start

**or**

tripping on the track?

WINNER: POINTS:

**Would you rather**

carry the torch for your country during the opening ceremonies

**or**

light the Olympic cauldron?

WINNER: POINTS:

**Would you rather**
be an Olympic coach
**or**
judge?

WINNER: POINTS:

**Would you rather**
get a private tour of
the Olympic Village
**or**
the training facilities?

WINNER: POINTS:

**Would you rather**

write a bestselling memoir
as an Olympic athlete

**or**

be an Olympian in a commercial
for a famous brand?

WINNER: POINTS:

**Would you rather**

hold the record for being the
youngest gold medalist

**or**

the oldest?

WINNER: POINTS:

**Would you rather**
run backward in the
100-meter hurdles
**or**
the relay?

WINNER: POINTS:

**Would you rather**
leave the Olympics without
any medals
**or**
have your biggest rival win five?

WINNER: POINTS:

**Would you rather**
run a marathon with a headache
**or**
an itchy rash?

WINNER: POINTS:

**Would you rather**
perform on the uneven bars with sticky tape on your hands
**or**
on a balance beam wearing slippers?

WINNER: POINTS:

**Would you rather**
be known for your flexibility
in gymnastics
**or**
strength?

WINNER: POINTS:

**Would you rather**
have an Olympic coach who is
unkind but knowledgeable
**or**
supportive and inexperienced?

WINNER: POINTS:

**Would you rather**
compete in long-distance running
**or**
short sprints?

WINNER: POINTS:

**Would you rather**
go into the Olympics as a talented underdog
**or**
a beloved athlete with high expectations from fans?

WINNER: POINTS:

**Would you rather**

get no sleep the night before your event

**or**

have a stomach virus?

WINNER: POINTS:

**Would you rather**

compete in a decathlon wearing flip-flops

**or**

clothes that are too tight?

WINNER: POINTS:

## TIEBREAKER

**Would you rather**

be a photographer at the Olympics

**or**

a commentator?

WINNER: POINTS:

# WINNER

WINNER: ______________________________

TOTAL POINTS: ______________________________

# ROUND 8

# Extreme Sports

**Would you rather**

jump out of a plane

**or**

climb Mount Everest?

WINNER: POINTS:

**Would you rather**

go whitewater rafting in the pouring rain

**or**

heli-skiing during a snowstorm?

WINNER: POINTS:

**Would you rather**

go BASE jumping off the Eiffel Tower on a windy day

**or**

the Empire State Building in the rain?

WINNER: POINTS:

**Would you rather**

descend into a canyon on a pulley system

**or**

free solo climb a mountain?

WINNER: POINTS:

**Would you rather**
go cliff diving in
shark-infested waters
**or**
parasailing through
a swarm of bees?

WINNER: POINTS:

**Would you rather**
go ice climbing in the Himalayas
**or**
descend into a deep cave?

WINNER: POINTS:

**Would you rather**

go rock climbing on a cold but clear day

**or**

a warm day with fog?

WINNER: POINTS:

**Would you rather**

go skydiving in tandem with someone who is terrified of heights

**or**

who gets airsick?

WINNER: POINTS:

**Would you rather**
bungee jump off a bridge
**or**
hang glide off a cliff?

WINNER: POINTS:

**Would you rather**
encounter strong winds while paragliding
**or**
get caught in a hailstorm?

WINNER: POINTS:

**Would you rather**
complete an obstacle course
on a dirt bike
**or**
a four-wheeler?

WINNER: POINTS:

**Would you rather**
mountain bike down a
trail with sharp turns
**or**
bumpy terrain?

WINNER: POINTS:

**Would you rather**
go hang gliding over a glacier
**or**
ancient ruins?

WINNER: POINTS:

**Would you rather**
try new snowboarding
tricks in a half-pipe
**or**
surf a huge wave?

WINNER: POINTS:

**Would you rather**

go wingsuit flying

**or**

free diving?

WINNER: POINTS:

**Would you rather**

ride down a volcano on a surfboard

**or**

a skateboard?

WINNER: POINTS:

**Would you rather**

sleep in a hammock dangling off the side of a mountain

**or**

in the highest tree in a rainforest?

WINNER: POINTS:

**Would you rather**

zip-line through the jungle using only one hand

**or**

bungee jump with only one leg strapped in?

WINNER: POINTS:

**Would you rather**
ride a sandboard that is ten feet long
**or**
two feet?

WINNER: POINTS:

**Would you rather**
drop into a busy skateboarding bowl with diarrhea
**or**
ski with a group down a steep slope while throwing up?

WINNER: POINTS:

## TIEBREAKER

**Would you rather**

ride over a waterfall
in a shopping cart

**or**

a plastic cooler?

WINNER: POINTS:

WINNER: ______________________________

TOTAL POINTS: ______________________________

WINNER
Would You
Rather?
SPORTS
EDITION

This certificate
is awarded to

______________________________

for being the captain of creativity, the first draft pick of funny responses, and the champion of cleverness. You're the MVP!

# CONGRATULATIONS!

# About the Author

**Lindsey Daly** grew up in Andover, New Jersey, and graduated from Ramapo College. She is a middle school social studies teacher and the author of the bestselling Would You Rather? series and card deck. She lives with her dogs, Teddy and Penny, in New Jersey.

Parents, for more information about Lindsey and her books, follow her online:

**@lindseydalybooks**

𝕏 **@LindseyDaly10**

Hi, Parents and caregivers,

We hope your child enjoyed *Would You Rather? Sports Edition*. If you have any questions or concerns about this book, or have received a damaged copy, please contact customerservice@penguinrandomhouse.com. We're here and happy to help. Also, please consider writing a review on your favorite retailer's website to let others know what you and your child thought of the book!

Sincerely,
The Zeitgeist Team

## DON'T MISS A SINGLE Would You Rather? QUESTION!

## FUN ALL YEAR ROUND

160+ silly scenarios: laugh, learn, and outsmart everyone

Fun competition and questions for the whole family

Start a competition and spirited conversations

## HOLIDAY AND SEASONAL LAUGHS

Enjoy egg-cellent Easter questions for everybunny

Join Santa and his elves for this super fun holiday game

Have fun, relax, and laugh with hilarious summer scenarios

**Parents, learn more about these books and upcoming titles at our "Would You Rather?" website.**

zeitgeistpublishing.com/wouldyourather